C000092499

Author: Yussuf Hamad BSc. Eng, MBA Finance

THIS BOOK BELONGS TO:	
SCHOOL	
CLASS	
YEAR	

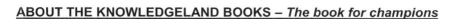

ABOUT THE KNOWLEDGELAND BOOKS – *The book for champions*

The main objective of **theknowledgeland books** is to deliver the ideas **step-by-step** from **basic** to the **competitive** level in the most **effective** and **efficient** way in order to guarantees **good results** and build the **confidence**.

Key words have been **bolded** throughout theknowledgeland books to boost **efficiency** and enhance **retention**.

To the parents / guardians

Go along with pupil from chapter to chapter assuring their **comprehension** while promoting the **independency**. Consequently, the independent reader becomes the best self-teacher and pupils should believe that: **THE BEST TEACHER IS THEMSELVES**.

Always try to teach yourself new things – **SELF DEVELOPMENT**.

LEVEL OF INDEPENDENCY

Year 1 and 2:   Go with pupil hand by hand through the book.

Year 3 and 4:   Go with pupil through **Examples** and encourage them

to do practice by themselves.

Year 5 and 6:   Encourage pupil to read and understand **Examples**

before doing practice questions.

KS3:   Encourage independency.

GCSE: Encourage independency.

How to use this book

Start from the beginning and go through topics in order of their appearance as the topic might use the knowledge of previous topic(s).

Repeat the topic if necessary.

THEKNOWLEDGELAND BOOKS – BOOKS FOR CHAMPS
www.theknowledgeland.co.uk

	BOOK NAME	ISBN NUMBER
1	PRE-SCHOOL (AGE 4 - 5)	B08JH3M42F
2	MATH YEAR 1 (AGE 5 - 6)	B08F9W214L
3	ENGLISH YEAR 1 (AGE 5 - 6)	B08FP4MN8S
4	PRACTICE BOOK MATH YEAR 1	B08MSLX63L
5	PRACTICE BOOK ENGLISH YEAR 1	
6	MATH YEAR 2 (AGE 6 - 7)	B08F6Y3VYR
7	ENGLISH YEAR 2 (AGE 6 - 7)	B08FBMFBDD
8	PRACTICE BOOK MATH YEAR 2	B08MSLX53V
9	PRACTICE BOOK ENGLISH YEAR 2	
10	MATH KS1 (AGE 5 - 7)	B08F6JZC46
11	ENGLISH KS1 (AGE 5 - 7)	B08F7VFTST
12	MATH YEAR 3 (AGE 7 - 8)	B08F6JZC52
13	ENGLISH YEAR 3 (AGE 7 - 8)	B08FKS7Y73
14	PRACTICE BOOK MATH YEAR 3	B08MRW6MYZ
15	PRACTICE BOOK ENGLISH YEAR 3	B08TZMKBQH
16	MATH YEAR 4 (AGE 8 - 9)	B08F6QNWHJ
17	ENGLISH YEAR 4 (AGE 8 - 9)	B08F7YWTX9
18	PRACTICE BOOK MATH YEAR 4	B08MSGQP2G
19	PRACTICE BOOK ENGLISH YEAR 4	B08TQ2QNBP
20	MATH YEAR 5 (AGE 9 - 10)	B08F6RCCLN
21	ENGLISH YEAR 5 (AGE 9 - 10)	B08F7QL781
22	PRACTICE BOOK MATH YEAR 5	B08MSLXH5G
23	PRACTICE BOOK ENGLISH YEAR 5	B08TT98SVG
24	MATH YEAR 6 (AGE 10 - 11)	B08F7VFTST
25	ENGLISH YEAR 6 (AGE 10 - 11)	B08F7GP4NS
26→	**PRACTICE BOOK MATH YEAR 6**	**B08MSQ3TJP**
27	PRACTICE BOOK ENGLISH YEAR 6	B08TQ9KSR3
28	MATH KS2 (AGE 7 - 11)	B08F6MVKYR
29	ENGLISH KS2 (AGE 7 - 11)	B08FKQNL1R
30	MATH KS3 (AGE 11 - 14)	B08F65SBM7
31	ENGLISH KS3 (AGE 11 - 14)	
32	PRACTICE BOOK MATH KS3	
33	PRACTICE BOOK ENGLISH KS3	
34	MATH GCSE (AGE 14 - 16)	B08F6MVL8K
35	PRACTICE BOOK MATH GCSE	

THE CONTENTS   PAGE NUMBERS

1. Counting to billion   1
2. Missing number   2
3. Pairs of numbers making 1,000,000,000   3
4. Trend   4
5. Numbers in Romans   5
6. Additions and subtractions   6
7. Time tables   10
8. Divisions   15
9. Fractions   21
10. Decimals   29
11. Percentages   35
12. BODMAS   41
13. The system   42
14. Ratio and proportion   43
15. Rounding   47
16. Algebra   49
     Expansions and factorization   51
     Equations   58
     Two equations   61
17. Problem solving   64
18. Measurements   74
19. Shapes and areas   77
20. Angles   83
21. Co-ordinates   86
22. Transformation   88
23. Handling data   91
     QUESTION BANK   94
     ANSWERS TO PRACTICES   100
     ANSWERS TO QUESTION BANK   126
     MINI FLASH CARDS   128

PRACTICE 1: COUNTING TO BILLION

Write the following numbers in words	
957,735,173,762	
Write the following words in numerals	
Eighty two billion, four hundred and sixty seven million, five hundred thousand, six hundred and seventy five	
5.5 billion	
6.8 million	
Nine trillion	
2.5k	

PRACTICE 2: MISSING NUMBERS

Fill in the missing numbers in the number lines below:

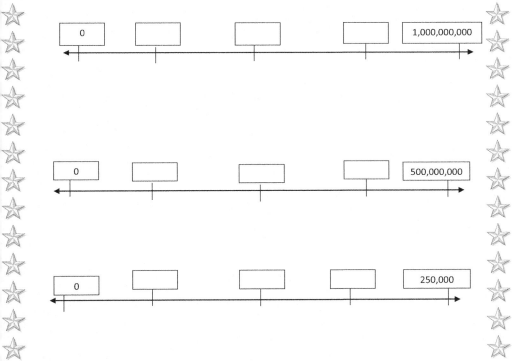

PRACTICE 3: PAIRS OF NUMBERS MAKING 1,000,000,000

Find the other pair of number which add up to 1,000,000,000

7,000,000	+	⬭	=	1,000,000,000
3,000,000	+	⬭	=	1,000,000,000
200,000	+	⬭	=	1,000,000,000
⬭	+	9,000,000	=	1,000,000,000
⬭	+	350,000	=	1,000,000,000
400	+	⬭	=	1,000,000,000
⬭	+	80,000	=	1,000,000,000
1	+	⬭	=	1,000,000,000

PRACTICE 4: TREND

Each line below, follow the specific rule to obtain the next number.

<u>State the rule</u> and <u>fill in</u> the missing numbers.

1	10	19	28		
Rule:					
42	34	26	18		
Rule:					
2	6	18	54		
Rule:					
100,000	50,000	25,000			
Rule:					
1	2	4	7	11	
Rule:					

PRACTICE 5: NUMBERS IN ROMANS

Standard	In numerals
653	
	MCMLXXIII
1234	
	XVI
2050	
	MCMIX
2022	

PRACTICE 6: ADDITIONS AND SUBTRACTIONS

Work out the following:

(1)
```
   5  6  2
+  3  4  9
_____
```

(2)
```
   4  8  5
+     5  6
_____
```

(3)
```
   7  3  8
+        7
_____
```

(4) Find the missing numbers.

```
    2  4  □
+  4  □  7
_____
   □  1  0
```

(5)
```
   6 ☐ 5
 +☐ 7 ☐
 ─────────
   9 0 1
```

Work out the following:

(6)
```
   8 1 5
 - 4 4 7
 ─────────
 ─────────
```

(7)
```
   3 1 4
 -   8 7
 ─────────
 ─────────
```

Find the missing numbers

(8)
```
   ☐ 3 5
 - 2 ☐ 7
 ─────────
   3 8 ☐
```

Work out the following:

(1) $12 - 21 =$

(2) $42 - 589 =$

(3) $1000 - 57 =$

(4) $498 + 75 =$

(5) $14 - 20 =$

Work out the following:

(1) 465 + $\bigcirc$ = 800

(2) $\bigcirc$ - 59 = 562

(3) 786 - $\bigcirc$ = 438

(4) 846 - $\bigcirc$ = 145

(5) 689 - $\bigcirc$ = 32

PRACTICE 9 : TIME TABLES

Work out the following:

9	X	4	=	
5	X	7	=	
8	X	6	=	
7	X	5	=	
9	X	8	=	
8	X	7	=	
9	X	7	=	
8	X	4	=	
7	X	6	=	
9	X	6	=	
4	X	8	=	
9	X	5	=	
8	X	5	=	
9	X	4	=	
7	X	3	=	
9	X	3	=	
8	X	8	=	
9	X	9	=	
7	X	4	=	

PRACTICE 10: MULTIPLICATION

Work out the following:

(1)   9 6 3

    x   7

    _____

(2)   3 8

    x   9 6

   +_____

    _____

(3)   5 6 4

    x   3 7

   +_____

    _____

Work out the following:

(4) 693 x 8 = ⬭

(5) 56 x 47 = ⬭

(6) 468 x 75 = ⬭

Fill in the following multiplication time grid.

(7)

X	9	⬭
8	⬭	56
⬭	54	⬭

(8)

X	⬭	⬭
8	32	48
⬭	⬭	30

Say whether statements are True of False.

(9) $19 \times 6 = (10 + 9) \times 6$ ☐

(10) $29 \times 8 = (30 - 1) \times 8 = 240 - 8$ ☐

Find out the missing number

(11) $72 \times 8 = 72 \times 10 - 72 \times$ ☐

Work out the following:

(12) $59 \times 84 =$

(13) $563 \times 74 =$

Say whether the following statements are True of False.

(14) $43 \times 20 = 43 \times 2 \times 10$ ☐

(15) $63 \times 30 = 63 \times 15 + 15$ ☐

(16) $99 \times 11 = 990 + 99$ ☐

Work out the following [as quickest way as you can]:

(17) $9800 \times 120 =$ ☐

(18) $90 \times 80 \times 50 =$ ☐

(19) $5 \times 68 \times 2 =$ ☐

(20) $50 \times 94 \times 2 =$ ☐

PRACTICE 11: SIMPLE DIVISION

Work out the following:

81	÷	9	=	
24	÷	8	=	
21	÷	3	=	
45	÷	5	=	
56	÷	7	=	
42	÷	6	=	
63	÷	9	=	
32	÷	8	=	
35	÷	7	=	
54	÷	6	=	
40	÷	8	=	
28	÷	7	=	
72	÷	9	=	
48	÷	6	=	
30	÷	6	=	
36	÷	9	=	
24	÷	4	=	
27	÷	3	=	
18	÷	6	=	
64	÷	8	=	

PRACTICE12: DIVISION WITHOUT REMAINDER

Work out the following:

(1) $\dfrac{400}{8} =$ ◯

(2) $\dfrac{720}{9} =$ ◯

(3) $\dfrac{4200}{70} =$ ◯

(4) $\dfrac{6300}{90} =$ ◯

(5) $\dfrac{4500}{90} =$ ◯

(6) $\dfrac{8412}{4} =$ ◯

(7) $\dfrac{4200}{60} =$ ◯

(8) $\dfrac{3500}{70}$ =

(9) $\dfrac{6005}{5}$ =

(10) $\dfrac{640480}{80}$ =

(11) $59\,\overline{)19352}$

(12) $27\,\overline{)14202}$

PRACTICE 13: DIVISION WITH REMAINDER

Work out the following:

(1) $\dfrac{100}{6} =$ _____ Remainder _____

(2) $\dfrac{100}{7} =$ _____ Remainder _____

(3) $\dfrac{100}{8} =$ _____ Remainder _____

(4) $\dfrac{402}{5} =$ _____ Remainder _____

(5) $\dfrac{400}{3} =$ _____ Remainder _____

PRACTICE 14: NUMBERS

(1) Write down the factors of:

    (a) 50

    (b) 60

(2) Find the HCF of:

    (a) 45 and 30

    (b) 30, 40 and 50

(3) Calculate the prime factors of:

    (a) 120

    (b) 180

(4) What is the HFC of:

    (a) $2 \times 3 \times 5$ and $2^2 \times 3 \times 5$

    (b) $2^3 \times 3 \times 5$ and $2^2 \times 3^3 \times 5$

(5) What is the LCM of:

    (a) $2 \times 3 \times 5$ and $2^3 \times 5$

    (b) $2^2 \times 3^2 \times 5^3$ and $2^3 \times 3 \times 5^2$

(6) Write down the multiple of 6 between 20 and 70.

(7) Find the LCM of:

  (a) 4 and 8

  (b) 6 and 9

  (c) 4, 5 and 6

(8) Find the values of:

  (a) $8^2 + 36 =$

  (b) $4^3 + 36 =$

(9) List down the prime numbers which are less than 30.

(10) List down the square numbers which are less than 30.

(11) List down the cube numbers which are less than 30.

(1) Draw any shape and shade the area $\frac{5}{8}$.

(2) What fraction is the following shaded area?

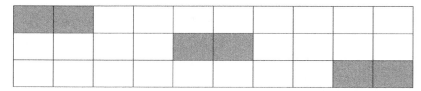

(3) <u>Fill in</u> the following table:

Mixed fraction	Improper fraction
	$\frac{25}{4}$
$3\frac{5}{6}$	

(4) Write the following fractions in their simplest form.

(a) $\frac{18}{72}$ = ⬭

(b) $\frac{21}{56}$ = ⬭

(c) $\frac{24}{32}$ = ⬭

(5) <u>Fill in</u> the missing numbers so that the
following fractions are equivalent.

(a) $\dfrac{}{3}$, $\dfrac{14}{}$, $\dfrac{16}{24}$

(b) $\dfrac{4}{}$, $\dfrac{24}{30}$, $\dfrac{}{45}$

(6) Arrange the following fractions from the
lowest to the highest.

$\dfrac{7}{10}$ $\dfrac{2}{5}$ $\dfrac{1}{2}$

(7) Arrange the following fractions from the
highest to the lowest.

$\dfrac{1}{5}$ $\dfrac{3}{10}$ $\dfrac{1}{4}$

(8) Which of the following fractions is equivalent to $\frac{6}{7}$?

    (a) $\frac{12}{35}$ (b) $\frac{18}{21}$ (c) $\frac{24}{48}$

(9) Which of the following fractions is <u>not</u> equivalent to $\frac{5}{6}$?

    (a) $\frac{25}{30}$ (b) $\frac{35}{42}$ (c) $\frac{30}{48}$

(10) Tick whether the following statement is True or False.

Statement	True	False
$8 = \frac{1}{8}$		
$9 = \frac{9}{1}$		
$\frac{4}{5} = \frac{4}{5} \times \frac{7}{7}$		
$\frac{3}{8} = \frac{3}{8} \div \frac{5}{5}$		

(11) Work out the following:

(i) $\dfrac{2}{3} + \dfrac{1}{3} = \boxed{}$

(ii) $\dfrac{1}{2} + \dfrac{1}{4} = \boxed{}$

(iii) $\dfrac{1}{6} - \dfrac{1}{8} = \boxed{}$

(iv) $\dfrac{2}{7} + \dfrac{4}{9} = \boxed{}$

(v) $1 + \dfrac{1}{6} = \boxed{}$

(vi) $3\dfrac{1}{2} - 1\dfrac{3}{4} = \boxed{}$

(vii) $\dfrac{1}{2} + \dfrac{1}{3} + \dfrac{1}{4} = \boxed{}$

Work out the missing fraction:

(viii) $\dfrac{1}{5} + \underline{} = 1$

24

(ix) $\frac{1}{7} + - = \frac{1}{6}$

(x) $3 - - = \frac{1}{8}$

(xi) $\frac{2}{5} + - + \frac{1}{4} = 1$

(12) Work out the followings:

(i) $\frac{2}{3} \; x \; \frac{9}{10} =$ ☐

(ii) $1\frac{1}{9} \; x \; \frac{3}{5} =$ ☐

(iii) $8 \; x \; \frac{3}{4} =$ ☐

(iv) $\frac{54}{63} \; x \; \frac{14}{72} =$ ☐

(v) $\dfrac{2}{5} \div \dfrac{4}{15} = \boxed{}$

(vi) $1\dfrac{1}{6} \ x \ \dfrac{1}{5} = \boxed{}$

(13) Write down the missing fraction

(i) $\dfrac{5}{6} \ x - = \dfrac{2}{3}$

(ii) $- \div \dfrac{4}{9} = \dfrac{27}{12}$

(iii) $\dfrac{1}{2} \ x \ \dfrac{2}{3} \ x - = \dfrac{4}{5}$

PRACTICE 16: MORE PRACTICE

Work out the following:

(1) $\frac{1}{4} + \frac{1}{4} =$ ☐

(2) $\frac{2}{15} + \frac{1}{5} =$ ☐

(3) $\frac{2}{3} + \frac{3}{4} =$ ☐

(4) $1\frac{1}{2} + 2\frac{3}{4} =$ ☐

(5) $2\frac{1}{5} - 1\frac{3}{10} =$ ☐

(6) $3\frac{1}{5} - 1\frac{2}{5} =$ ☐

(7) $\frac{2}{25} \ x \ 7\frac{1}{2} =$ ☐

(8) $\frac{18}{12} \ x \ \frac{8}{6} =$ ☐

(9) $\dfrac{1}{10} \times \dfrac{15}{2} =$ ☐

(10) $\dfrac{4}{5} \div \dfrac{2}{15} =$ ☐

(11) $3\dfrac{3}{4} \div \dfrac{5}{8} =$ ☐

PRACTICE 17: DECIMALS

(1) Place <, > or = to make the following statements correct.

0.2		0.02
0.5		0.50
0.3		0.30
0.07		0.6
0.9		0.10
0.08		0.80
0.12		0.21

(2) Arrange the following numbers from the lowest to the highest.

0.9   0.10   0.11   0.300   0.80

(3) Tick whether the following statements are True of False.

Statement	True	False
$0.01 = \dfrac{0.1}{100}$		
$0.03 = \dfrac{3}{100}$		
$0.6 \times 0.7 = \dfrac{6 \times 7}{100}$		
$\dfrac{0.8 \times 0.9}{0.1} = \dfrac{8 \times 9}{100}$		

(4) Work out the following:

(i)　　$0.8 + 0.9 =$

(ii)　　$0.68 + 1.7 =$

(iii)　　$4.15 + 9 =$

(iv)　　$1.90 - 0.34 =$

(v)　　$1 + 0.25 =$

(5) Work out the following:

(i) $0.3 \times 4 =$ ⬭

(ii) $0.5 \times 0.6 =$ ⬭

(iii) $9 \times 1.8 =$ ⬭

(iv) $6.7 \times 8.9 =$ ⬭

(v) $1.2 \times 400 =$ ⬭

(vi) $0.36 \div 4 =$ ⬭

(vii) $1.23 \div 3 =$ ⬭

(viii) $4.836 \div 6 =$ ⬭

(ix) $4.2 \div 800 =$ ⬭

(x) $4.2 \div 700 =$ ⬭

PRACTICE 18: MORE PRACTICE

(1) Change the following <u>decimals into fractions</u>:

   (i) $0.35 =$ ⬭

   (ii) $0.05 =$ ⬭

(2) Change the following <u>fractions into decimals</u>:

   (i) $\dfrac{4}{5} =$ ⬭

   (ii) $\dfrac{1}{50} =$ ⬭

(3) Work out the following. Give the answers in fraction and in decimals.

	In fraction	In decimal
$1\dfrac{1}{2} + 2\dfrac{1}{4}$		
$3\dfrac{2}{5} - 1\dfrac{3}{5}$		

$\dfrac{1}{4} \times \dfrac{2}{5}$		
$2\dfrac{1}{2} \times \dfrac{1}{10}$		
$\dfrac{3}{4} \div 1\dfrac{1}{4}$		

(4) State whether the following statements are true or false.

$\dfrac{0.03}{0.03} = \dfrac{3}{3}$	
$\dfrac{0.05}{0.5} = \dfrac{5}{5}$	
$\dfrac{0.12}{0.15} = \dfrac{12}{15}$	
$\dfrac{0.01}{0.1} = \dfrac{1}{10}$	
$\dfrac{0.12}{0.6} = \dfrac{12}{60}$	

(5) Work out the following:

(i) $\dfrac{0.3}{0.03} =$

(ii) $\dfrac{0.12}{0.06}$ =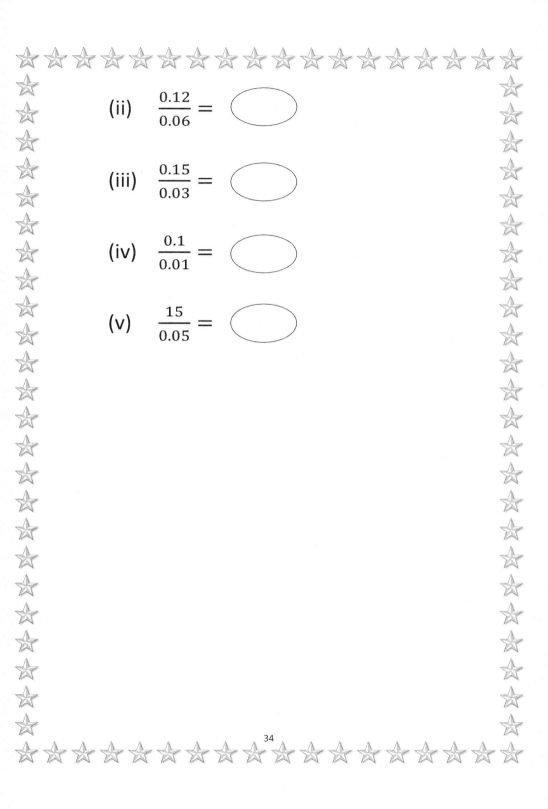

(iii) $\dfrac{0.15}{0.03}$ =

(iv) $\dfrac{0.1}{0.01}$ =

(v) $\dfrac{15}{0.05}$ =

PRACTICE 19: PERCENTAGES

(1) The rectangle below contains 14 donut shapes and 6 triangle shapes.

(a) Which of the following equations can be used to find the percentage of triangle in a box?

(i) percentage of triangle = $\frac{number\ of\ triangles}{total\ number\ of\ shapes}$ x 100%

(ii) percentage of triangle = $\frac{total\ number\ of\ shapes}{number\ of\ triangles}$ x 100%

(b) Calculate the percentage of triangle shapes in a box.

(c) Calculate the percentage of donut shapes in a box.

(2) In a box, there are 12 chocolate cakes and 28 toffee cakes.

   (i)   What is the percentage of chocolate cakes in a box? ☐

   (ii) What is the percentage of toffee cakes in a box? ☐

(3) There are some people in a whole. 25% are teachers and the rest are students. There are 10 teachers in a whole. How many students are there? ☐

(4) There are 20 cars in a show room of which 3 are convertible. What is the percentage of non convertible cars in a room? ☐

(5) 52% of the students in a physics class were girls. There were 26 girls in a class. How many students were there altogether? ☐

(6) Fill in the following table:

Fractions	Decimal	Percentage
		80%
	0.12	
$\dfrac{13}{100}$		
		20%
	0.45	
$\dfrac{1}{20}$		

(7) Arrange the following numbers from the highest to the lowest.

0.5, $\dfrac{1}{10}$, $\dfrac{4}{5}$,   0.3

(8) Arrange the following numbers from the lowest to the highest.

$\frac{9}{10}$,   0.4, $\frac{7}{10}$,   0.2, $\frac{3}{5}$

(9) 50kg has increased by 30%
How much (kg) it would be? ☐

(10) Ali said if 40$ increased by 20% and then decreased by 20%, the result will be 40$ as before. ☐
Is Ali correct? Show your workings.

(11) Knowing that:

Sale Price = Original Price – Discount

The original price of the trainers was 50€.

The seller offers 30% discount.

(i)   How much is the discount? ☐

(ii)   What is the sale price? ☐

(12)   The train ticket was £12 in 2020.
The train ticket fare increased by 2% in 2021.
How much was the train fare in 2021?

‎ ‎

(13)   In 2020, UK population was 65 million.
The male percentage was 45%.
How many female were there?

(14)   Palmer sports club offers 4 types of sports – football, basket ball, rugby and cricket.
The club has 200 members.
40% play football, 25% play basket ball, 20% play rugby and the rest play cricket.
How many members play cricket?

(15) Students from English class have been asked which transport they use to go to school.

Here is the result:

Type of transport	Number of students
Bus	20
Car	12
Walk	
Tax	3
Total	50

What percentage of the students who are walking to school?

PRACTICE 20: BODMAS

Work out the following:

(1) $(59 - 39) \div \frac{5}{3} =$ ☐

(2) $3(\frac{500}{4} - 25) =$ ☐

(3) $(47 + 13) \times 70\% =$ ☐

(4) $\frac{2}{1+(10-3)} \times 4 =$ ☐

(5) $4 + (10 - 4) \times 1.5 =$ ☐

(6) $5 + (12 - 8) \times \frac{32}{48} \times 2 =$ ☐

(7) $6 + 3 \times 2 =$ ☐

(8) $7 \times 4 - 3 =$ ☐

(9) $8 \times 5 - 3 \times 4 =$ ☐

(10) $8 \times (5 - 3) \times 4 =$ ☐

The system has **input, process and output**.

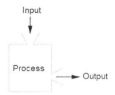

(1) Write down the <u>process</u> if inputs are:
20, 2, 4 and 10 to get the result = 100.

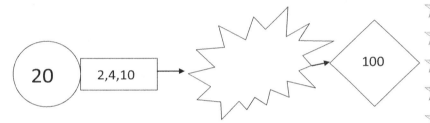

(2) Write down the <u>process</u> if inputs are:
40, 2, 3 and 8 to get the result = 30.

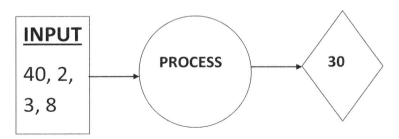

PRACTICE 22: RATIO AND PROPORTION

Consider the line below:

A   B   C

(1) The ratio of the line AB:BC = 4:1

The length AC = 600 cm.

Calculate the length:

     (i)   AB

     (ii)   BC

AB =

BC =

(2) The ratio of the line BC:AC = 2:7

The length BC = 14 ft.

Calculate the length:

     (i)   AB

     (ii)   AC

AB =

AC =

(3) The rectangular model of the football field has length = 6cm and width = 2.5cm.

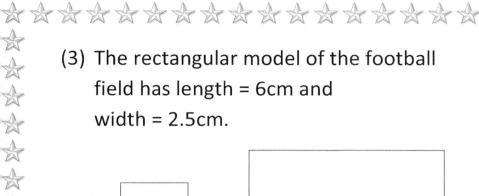

2.5cm

6cm

120cm

The actual field has length = 120cm.

Calculate the width of the actual field.

(4) The model of the square room is one-hundredth of the actual room.
The model has sides = 7cm.
What are the sides of the actual room in metre?

(5) In the 5000-litre pond, there are new born baby toads distributed evenly throughout the pond.

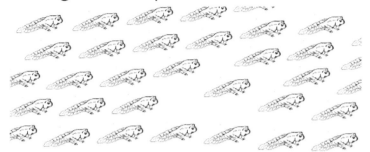

500ml sample of water was taken from the pond and there were 15 baby toads. Estimate the number of baby toads in the pond.

(6) The drink contains 20g of sugar in 200ml.

    (i)   What would be the sugar content in 1.5 litre of a drink? _____g

    (ii)   What is the amount of drink which would contain 75g of sugar? __mls

(7) The scale of the map is 1:100,000.

scale 1:100,000

The distance from A to B on the map is 6cm. What is the actual distance on the ground? _____km

PRACTICE 23: ROUNDING

(1) Round the following numbers:

Round to:	Nearest digits
5.4	
$7\frac{3}{4}$	
Round to:	Nearest tens
46	
73	
Round to:	Nearest hundreds
539	
262	
Round to:	Nearest thousands
5,464	
4,820	
Round to:	Nearest ten thousands
24,642	
82,976	
Round to:	Nearest millions
2,612,431	
7,429,658	

(2) Round to the nearest:

Round 6,735,829 to the nearest:	
Million:	
Ten thousand	
Thousand	
Hundred	
Ten	

PRACTICE 24: ALGEBRA

Simplify the following:

(1) $a + a + a + b + b =$

(2) $4a + 5b - 7a - 7b =$

(3) $2a + 6b - 5a - 5 =$

Work out the following:

(4) $20 \times a =$

(5) $2b \times 3b =$

(6) $16 \times \dfrac{3b}{4} =$

(7) $3a \times 4bc =$

(8) $\dfrac{4ab}{2b} =$

(9) $\dfrac{4a^2b}{2ab^2} =$

(10) $\dfrac{4a \; x \; 5b}{20a} =$

(11) $\dfrac{(a+b) \; x \; (a \; x \; b)}{(a+b)} =$

(12) $\dfrac{(a+b)+ (a+b)+ (a+b)}{a+b} =$

(13) $\dfrac{4b^2}{2b} =$

(14) $\dfrac{4(a+b)^2}{2(a+b)} =$

PRACTICE 25: EXPANSIONS AND FACTORIZATIONS

(1) Expand the following and simplify if possible.

(i) $a(b + c) = $

(ii) $3a(4b - 2c) = $

(iii) $(m + n)(m - n) = $

(iv) $(2p + 3)(4p - 5) = $

(v) $(a + b)(a + b) = $

(vi) $(a + b)(a - b) = $

(vii) $3(a + \dfrac{2b}{9}) = $

(viii) $12(b - \dfrac{5c}{4}) = $

(2) Factorize the following:

    (i) $ab + ac =$ $\boxed{}$

    (ii) $3abc - 6ac =$ $\boxed{}$

    (iii) $12ab^2 + 6a^2b =$ $\boxed{}$

    (iv) $3ab - 12ab^2 =$ $\boxed{}$

    (v) $4a^2b^2c + 20abc =$ $\boxed{}$

(3) Work out the following:

    (i)   Expand: $5(a + \frac{b}{10})$ $\boxed{}$

    (ii)   Write down the missing number

         $7a + b = 7($ $+$ $)$

(4) Simplify following:

    (i) $\dfrac{4a+8b}{2a+4b} =$ ⬚

    (ii) $\dfrac{5a+20b+a-2b}{4a+10b-a-b} =$ ⬚

(5) Tick whether the following statements are True of False.

Statement	True	False
A + B = B + A		
A − B = B − A		
A x B = B x A		
$\dfrac{A}{B} = \dfrac{B}{A}$		
$\dfrac{A + B}{B} = A$		

$$\frac{A \times B}{A} = B$$		
$$\frac{4a + 5b}{4a} = \frac{4a}{4a} + 5b$$		
$$\frac{4a + 5b}{4a} = \frac{4a}{4a} + \frac{5b}{4a}$$		
$$\frac{6a \times b}{c} = \frac{6a}{c} \times \frac{b}{c}$$		
$$\frac{6a \times b}{c} = \frac{6a}{c} \times b$$		

PRACTICE 26: EXPRESSIONS

(1) If m = 2 and n = 5, write down the values of the following expressions:

(i) $3m - n = $ ☐

(ii) $\dfrac{3n - 3m}{n - m} = $ ☐

(iii) $\dfrac{5n - 2m}{m + n} - 3 = $ ☐

(iv) $\dfrac{(m+1)(n+1)}{n + m} \times 28 = $ ☐

(v) $\dfrac{m^2 + n^2}{m + n} = $ ☐

(2) If X and Y are the two numbers such that X > Y.

Write down the expressions according to the following statements:

Statement	Expression
The sum of two numbers	
The difference of two numbers	
The product of two numbers	
The first number is three times the second number	

(3) Let M be the money in your pocket. Write down the expressions that can calculate the amount of money in your pocket according to the following statements:

Statement	Expression
You had £50 and you gave some money away	
You had some money and you gave £5 away	
You had some money and you add the same amount of money into your pocket	
You had money and you add half of the amount of money you had into your pocket	

PRACTICE 27: EQUATIONS

Solve the following equations:

(1) $192 + x = 243$ $\rightarrow x =$

(2) $497 - 2x = 321$ $\rightarrow x =$

(3) $\frac{q}{70} = 80$ $\rightarrow q =$

(4) $2q + 35 = 9q$ $\rightarrow q =$

(5) $1 + \frac{q}{4} = 5$ $\rightarrow q =$

(6) $\frac{5q}{4} + \frac{1}{4} = \frac{1}{3}$ $\rightarrow q =$

(7) $\frac{12+q}{q} = 5$ $\rightarrow q =$

(8) $2(4q + 5) + 10 = 36$ $\rightarrow q =$

(9) $\dfrac{25}{20+3q} = 1$ $\rightarrow$ q =

(10) $\dfrac{2q+1}{3q-5} = \dfrac{7}{4}$ $\rightarrow$ q =

(11) Given that T = 50 + 4n

    (i) What is the value of T when n = 6? ▭

    (ii) What is the value of n when T = 170? ▭

Work out the following:

(12) If 3a + 6b = 30

    What is the value of a + 2b ▭

(13) If 2a + b = 1

    Find the value of $a + \dfrac{b}{2}$ ▭

(14) If 4p + 6q = 20

    Find the value of $p + \dfrac{3}{2}q$ ▭

(15) Equations are given and follow the instructions

    (i)   Equation: $12A + 3B = 9C$

        Instruction: Divide both sides by 3

    (ii)   Equation: $A + B = C$

        Instruction: Multiply both sides by 5

    (iii)   Equation: $\dfrac{A}{2} + B = C$

        Instruction: Multiply both sides by 2

    (iv)   Equation: $\dfrac{3A}{2} + \dfrac{5B}{4} = \dfrac{5C}{8}$

        Instruction: Multiply both sides by 2

    (v)   Equation: $\dfrac{3A}{4} + \dfrac{5B}{2} = \dfrac{4C}{3}$

        Instruction: Multiply both sides by 12

In the pair of equations below, find the values of p and r.

(1) $4p = 12$ p =

     $3p + r = 11$ r =

(2) $6p = 1.8$ p =

     $2p + r = 0.8$ r =

(3) $\dfrac{80}{p} = 20$ p =

     $2p + 3r = 23$ r =

(4) $\dfrac{p}{3} + \dfrac{2p}{3} = 1$ p =

     $2p + 5r = 22$ r =

(5) 20% of p = 24   p =

     30% of p + 40% of r = 96   r =

(6) 20p = 1000   p =

4p + 5r = 7700   r =

Answer the following questions:

(7) If A + B = X

A − B = Y

Then, which of the two equations

below are true?

	Tick two
(a) A + B = X + Y	
(b) 2A = X + Y	
(c) 2A + 2B = X + Y	
(d) A = $\frac{X+Y}{2}$	

(8) A + B = 20

A − B = 10

A =

B =

(9) 3 pencils cost £1.20

2 pencils and one rubber cost £1.00

Cost of one pencil = ☐

Cost of one rubber = ☐

(10) $\Omega + \Omega + \Omega + \Omega = 52$

$\alpha + \alpha + \Omega + \alpha + \alpha + \Omega = 58$

$\Omega =$

$\alpha =$

(11) The weight of 5 big blocks is equal to the weight of 6 small blocks.

The weight of one big block is 3 kg.

What is the weight of one small block?

☐

PRACTICE 29: PROBLEM SOLVING

GUESS MY NUMBER!

(1) I think of a number, then I add half of it to it, then I add quarter of it, the result is 175.

    (i)   Write down the equation to find the number. _____

    (ii)   What is the number I am thinking of? _____

(2) I think a number and I doubled it, then I add half of the number I thought of, then I add 10. The result is 20.

    (i)   Write down the equation to find the number. _____

    (ii)   What is the number I am thinking of? _____

THE COST TO FUNFAIR

(3) It cost £2 to enter into the funfair ground and it cost £3 for each ride you want to go into.

    (i)   Write down the equation to find the total cost to funfair.

    (ii)   If you want to go on 5 rides, how much you would need?

    (iii)   If you have £30, how many rides you would be able to go into?

(4) Given that the chicken need to be cooked for at least 30 minutes plus 25 minutes for each kg that the chicken weighs.

    (i)   Write down the equation which calculates the time for cooking the chicken.

                    ☐

    (ii)   If the chicken weighs 3kg, how long would it take to cook the chicken? ☐

    (iii)   It took 2 hours and 35 minutes to cook the chicken. How much the chicken weighs? ☐

(5) A teacher bought 15 pens for students. She paid £10 and she got back £5.5 change.

How much does each pen cost? ☐

(6) Bradley bought 3 apples for £1.20 and Kendis bought 2 apples and 2 bananas for £1.40.
How much each apple and each banana cost?

THE BEST BUY PROBLEM

(7) Bag "A" contains 5kg of rice and it costs £5.50. Bag "B" contains 3kg of rice and it costs £3.60.

Which one is the best buy?
Why?

PRACTICE 30: MORE PRACTICE

(1) Find the values of a and b if:

$$a = \frac{1}{2}b \qquad \text{and} \qquad a + b = 90$$

a =	b =

For questions 2 – 7:

(i)   Write down the equations according to the instructions.

(ii) Find the values of a and b.

(2) The sum of a and b is 40. b is three times of a.

(i)   Equations:

(ii) a =   b =

(3) The difference of a and b is 75. a is half of b.

(i) Equations:

(ii) a =   b =

(4) The sum of a and b is 450. a is double of b.

(i) Equations:

(ii) a =   b =

(5) The sum of a and b is 100. b is 20 less than a.

    (i)   Equations:

    (ii)   a =   b =

(6) The sum of a and b is 121. a is ten times of b.

    (i)   Equations:

    (ii)   a =   b =

(7) The sum of a and b is 70. a is 12 more than b.

   (i)   Equations:

   (ii)   a =   b =

(8) Jamal and Jaden together weight 80kg. Jaden alone weight 26kg.
How much does Jamal weigh?

(9) One bag of potatoes and one bag of rice both together cost £12. A bag of rice costs as three times as a bag of potatoes.

   (i)   How much is a bag of potatoes?

   (ii)   How much is a bag of rice?

(10) The sum of Salum's age and Fatmas age is 14 years. Fatma is 4 years younger than Salum.

(i) How old is Salum?

(ii) How old is Fatma?

(11) I bought 6 pens and 3 rubbers for £2.40. I then bought 3 rubbers for 60p. How much does each pen cost?

(12) There are two pieces of string: red and blue. The piece of blue string is 4 times longer than the piece of red string.

Two pieces of string are joined end to end. The total length is 20cm.

(i) How long is the red string?

(ii) How long is the blue string?

(13) The weight of strawberries' bag and the weight of grapes' bag is 3.4kg. The weight of strawberries' bag is 1.6kg less than the weight of grapes' bag.

(i) How much is the weight of strawberries' bag? ☐

(ii) How much is the weight of grapes' bag? ☐

[QUANTITIES AND UNITS]

(1) Match the quantity with their corresponding units.

Quantity	Units
Time	$kg \div \dfrac{kg}{m^3}$
Distance	$second \times \dfrac{metre}{second}$
Weight	$\dfrac{kg}{m^3} \times m^3$
Volume	$meter \div \dfrac{meter}{second}$
Money	$kg \div \dfrac{kg}{\$}$

(2) Given that 10€ = 12$

  (i) How much $ is 90€?   _____$

  (ii) How much € is 60$?   _____€

(3) Given that 10 miles = 16 kilometres (km)

  (i) How many km is 50 miles?   _____Km

  (ii) How many miles is 400km? _____km

(4) Given that 1 litre = 0.22 gallons

  (i)How many gallons is 10 litres? _gallons

  (ii)How many gallons is 100 litres?

  gallons

  Work out the following:

(5) 200g + 4kg = _____kg

(6) 0.3kg + 150g = _____g

(7) 0.1 litre + 250mls = _____mls

(8) 2 litres + 700mls = = _____litres

(9) £0.2 + 60p = _____p

(10) 80p + 75p =£ _____

(11) How many 20mls are in5 litres?

PRACTICE 32 SHAPES AND AREAS

(1) <u>Match</u> the type of triangle with their corresponding names.

Shape		Triangle name
		Equilateral
		Right angled
		Scalene
		Isosceles

(2) The area of big circle is 25cm^2 and the area of small circle is 12cm^2.

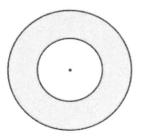

Calculate the <u>shaded area</u>. _____

(3) The circle is in the square whose sides are 14cm length.

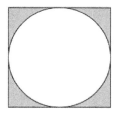

The area of the circle is 154cm^2.

Calculate:

(i)   The <u>shaded area</u>.
(ii) The <u>radius of the circle</u>. _____

(4) Four identical circles are in the square whose sides are 84m length.

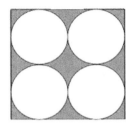

The area of each circle is 1386m^2.

Calculate:

(i)   The <u>shaded area</u>.

(ii) The <u>radius of the circle</u>.

(5) Calculate the <u>area</u> and the <u>perimeter</u> of the rectangle below.

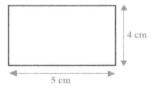

4 cm

5 cm

(6) Calculate the <u>area</u> and the <u>perimeter</u> of the right-angled triangle below.

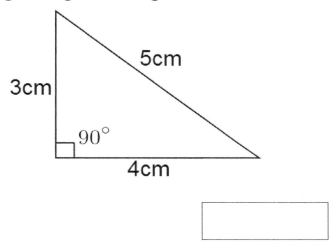

5cm

3cm

$90°$

4cm

(7) Calculate the <u>area</u> and <u>perimeter</u> of the figure below.

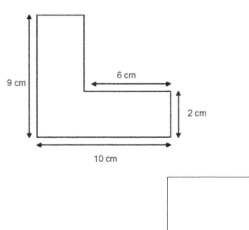

9 cm

6 cm

2 cm

10 cm

(8) The picture frame, ABCD, has a dimension of 20m by 15m.
A picture is placed on the frame leaving the space of 1m each side.

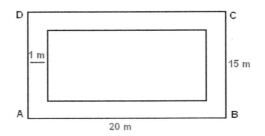

Calculate:
   (i)   The <u>area of the picture</u>.
   (ii)   The <u>perimeter of the picture</u>.

(9) The rectangle below has a perimeter of 28cm. Calculate its <u>area</u>.

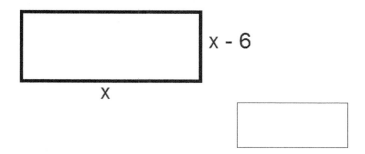

$x - 6$

x

(10) The rectangular table has perimeter of 50cm. Its length is 5cm more than its width.

Calculate the <u>area of the table</u>.

PRACTICE 33 ANGLES

(1) Match the angle and its type.

Angles		Type
		Obtuse angle
		Acute
		Right angle
		Reflex angle

(2) The pointer of the clock moved from "12" position.

What size of the angle the pointer would make if it would move to:

Clock face	Pointer moved:	Angle size
	12	
	1	
	7	

(3) How many degrees the pointer would make if it would move from "2" position to "7" position?

(4) Suppose you are walking toward North and then you turned toward East. What the size of angle you would have made?

(5) Suppose you are walking toward North and then you turned toward East, then toward South and last toward West. What the size of angle you would have made in total?

PRACTICE 34: CO-ORDINATES

(1) Look at the x-y plane below:

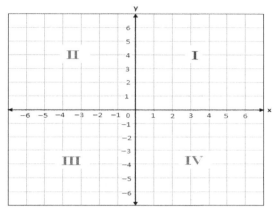

Match the signs of the co-ordinates with their corresponding quadrants.

Quadrant		Signs
I		(+x, +y)
II		(-x, +y)
III		(+x, -y)
IV		(-x, -y)

(2) The figure below is a square drawn on x-y plane. M is the midpoint of the diagonal.

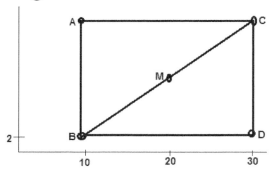

Write down the co-ordinates of the points A, B, C, D and M.

B(,   )

A(,   )

D(,   )

C(,   )

PRACTICE 35: TRANSFORMATION (reflection and translation)

Look at the figure below:

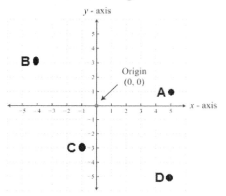

(1) Write the co-ordinates of the points A, B, C and D.

A(,) B(,) C(,) D(,)

(2) Write down the new co-ordinates if:

(i) Point A was reflected on x-axis.   A'(,)

(ii) Point B was reflected on y-axis.   B'(,)

(iii) Point C was reflected on
x-axis.   C'(,)

(iv) Point D was reflected on
y-axis.   D'(,)

(3) Write down the new co-ordinates
if the points are translated by:

(i) Point A: 2 units left and 3
units up.   A'(,)

(ii) Point B: 6 units right and 8
units down.   B'(,)

(iii) Point C: 2 units right and 1
unit up.   C'(,)

(iv) Point D: 1 unit left and 2
units up.   D'(,)

(4)   Look at the figure below:

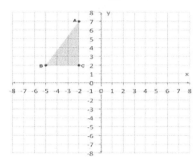

The triangle ABC was reflected on y-axis.

Plot the triangle on its new position.

(5)   Look at the figure below:

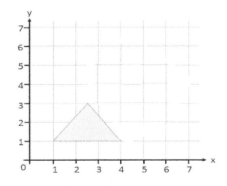

The triangle above has been translated by: 2 units right and 3 units above.

Plot the triangle on its new position.

PRACTICE 36: HANDLING DATA

(1) Match the items.

Data you collected from the internet		Primary Data
Data you collected from the library		Secondary data
You counted and recorded the type of the car passing on the road		

(2)

Weight of students		Discrete Data
Number of the students		
Height of the plants		Continuous Data

91

(3) Ten students took the math test and altogether they got the total marks of 730 as follows:

70, 80, 90, 90, 80, 70, 60, 60, 50, 80

Calculate:

(a) Mean mark [ ]

(b) Median [ ]

(c) Mode and [ ]

(d) Range [ ]

(e) The above information was put in a tally table. Complete the table.

Marks	Tally	frequency

(f) Represent the above information in a bar chart.

(4) Look at the pictogram below:

How many children chose cottage pie?

QUESTION BANK

Work out the following:

(1) 2439 + 638 =

(2) 1,000,000 − 1 =

(3) 5 − 8 =

(4) 72 − 123 =

(5) Write down the missing numbers

____, 26, 38, ____, 62, 74, ____.

(6) 42 x 53 =

(7) 8349 x 76 =

(8) 3832 ÷ 4 =

(9) 16638 ÷ 47 =

(10) 4263 - _____ = 798

(11) $\dfrac{1}{6} - \dfrac{1}{9} =$

(12) $\dfrac{4}{5} \div 28 =$

(13) $1\dfrac{2}{3} + 2\dfrac{3}{4} =$

(14) $2\dfrac{3}{5} x 25 =$

(15) $2\dfrac{1}{2} \div 1\dfrac{4}{5} =$

(16) 27 x 1.6 =

(17) 400 x 2.4 =

(18) 14.5 ÷ 4 =

(19) 1.45 ÷ 0.4 =

(20) 30% of £160 =

(21) The table below shows the temperature on the first of January.

Glasgow	London
-3°C	4°C

(i) What is the difference in temperature between London and Glasgow?

(ii) On the 15th of January, the temperature of Glasgow was 8° lower than that of the 1st of January.

What was the temperature of Glasgow on the 15th of January?

(22) Tick two digital reading that correspond to the clock reading

Clock reading	Digital reading	
	13:35	
	7:35	
	1:35	
	3:35	

(23) Work out the time you suppose to wake up for school so that you get to school on time.

Time spent to:	
Get prepared for school	30 minutes
Walk to school	15 minutes
Time you are suppose to be at school	08:45
Time to wake up	

(24) Add the following times:

    1 : 50   (1 hour and 50 minutes)

    2 : 45   (2hours 45 minutes)
    _____

    _____

(25) The bus times from Coley Park to Cemetery Junction is as follow:

Coley Park	07:13
Humble Court	07:25
Cemetery Junction	08:08

How long does the bus take from Coley Park to Cemetery Junction?

(26) Round the following number to the nearest tens.

	To the nearest tens
12.521	
125.21	
1252.1	

(27) Find the value of M if:

$$M - (1.25 + 1.6) = \frac{3}{4}M$$

(28) Rose had some money. She spent £2.20 for lunch and £1.80 for drink. She then left with two-third of the money the money she started with.

How much did she have at the start?

(29) Work out the values of x and y if:

3x = 96 and

2x + 2y = 100   x = ____ , y = ____ .

(30) Given that 6x = 24 and 3x − 4y = 2

Find the values of x and y.

x = ____ , y = ____ .

(31) Mbaraka bought 4 apples for 1.2$. Then he bought 2 apples and 3 bananas for 2.1$. how much each apple and each banana cost?   Apple ____$, banana __$

(32) The cable AB was 6cm long.

6cm

A   B

Ali cut 1.4cm and Khadija cut 2.3cm of the cable. What is the remaining length of the cable?

(33) Each bag of sweet cost 60p. Serena buys 4 bags of sweets. She paid £5. How much change she would get back?

(34) David buys 3 bags of chocolate. He paid £10 and he got back £7.90 change. How much each bag cost?

(35) Use the fact that 69 x 76 = 5,244 to find the values of (i) 69 x 77

(ii) 69 x 78

PRACTICE 1: COUNTING TO BILLION

957,735,173,762
Nine hundred and fifty seven billion, seven hundred and thirty five million, one hundred and seventy three thousand, seven hundred and sixty two
Eighty two billion, four hundred and sixty seven million, five hundred thousand, six hundred and seventy five. - 82,467,500,675
5.5 billion – 5,500,000,000
6.8 million – 6,800,000
Nine trillion - 9,000,000,000,000
2.5k – 2,500

PRACTICE 2: MISSING NUMBERS

250,000,000	500,000,000	750,000,000

125,000,000	250,000,000	375,000,000

62,500	125,000	187,500

PRACTICE 3: PAIRS OF NUMBERS MAKING 1,000,000,000

7,000,000	+	993000000	=	1,000,000,000
3,000,000	+	997000000	=	1,000,000,000
200,000	+	999800000	=	1,000,000,000
991000000	+	9,000,000	=	1,000,000,000
999650000	+	350,000	=	1,000,000,000
400	+		=	1,000,000,000
999920000	+	80,000	=	1,000,000,000
1	+	999999999	=	1,000,000,000

PRACTICE 4: TREND

1	10	19	28	37	46
Rule:+9					
42	34	26	18	10	2
Rule:-8					
2	6	18	54	162	486
Rule:x3					
100,000	50,000	25,000	12500	6250	3125
Rule: ÷2					
1	2	4	7	11	16
Rule:+1, +2, +3, +4, ...					

PRACTICE 5: NUMBERS IN ROMANS

Standard	In numerals
653	DCLIII
1973	MCMLXXIII
1234	MCCXXXIV
16	XVI
2050	MML
1909	MCMIX
2022	MMXXII

PRACTICE 6: ADDITIONS AND SUBTRACTIONS

(1)

```
   5¹  6¹  2
+  3   4   9
   9   1   1
```

(2)

```
   4   81  5
+      5   6
   5   4   1
```

(3)

```
   7   31  8
+          7
   7   4   5
```

(4)

```
   2¹  4¹  3
+  4   6   7
   7   1   0
```

(5)

```
   6   2   5
+  2   7   6
   9   0   1
```

(6)

```
   8   1   5
-  4   4   7
   3   6   8
```

(7)

```
   3   1   4
-      8   7
   2   2   7
```

(8)

```
   6   3   5
-  2   4   7
   3   8   8
```

PRACTICE 7: MORE PRACTICE

(1) $12 - 21 = -9$

(2) $42 - 589 = -547$

(3) $1000 - 57 = 943$

(4) $498 + 75 = 573$

(5) $14 - 20 = 6$

PRACTICE 8: MORE PRACTICE

(1) $465 + 335 = 800$

(2) $621 - 59 = 562$

(3) $786 - 348 = 438$

(4) $846 - 701 = 145$

(5) $689 - 657 = 32$

PRACTICE 9 : TIME TABLES

9	X	4	=	36
5	X	7	=	35
8	X	6	=	48
7	X	5	=	35
9	X	8	=	72
8	X	7	=	56
9	X	7	=	63
8	X	4	=	32
7	X	6	=	42
9	X	6	=	54
4	X	8	=	32
9	X	5	=	45
8	X	5	=	40
9	X	4	=	36
7	X	3	=	21
9	X	3	=	27
8	X	8	=	64
9	X	9	=	81
7	X	4	=	28

PRACTICE 10: MULTIPLICATION

(1)
```
    9   6   3
  x         7
  6 7   4   1
```

(2)
```
        3   8
    x   9   6
  3 4   2
+   2   2   8
  3 6   4   8
```

(3)
```
      5   6   4
  x       3   7
1 6   9   2
+   3   9   4   8
2   0   8   6   8
```

(4)   693 x 8 = 5544

(5)   56 x 47 = 2632

(6)   468 x 75 = 35100

(7)

X	9	7
8	**72**	56
6	54	**42**

(8)

X	4	6
8	56	72
5	**20**	54

(9)   19 x 6 = (10 + 9) x 6 (T)

(10)   29 x 8 = (30 − 1) x 8 = (T)

(11)   72 x 8 = 72 x 10 − 72 x **2**

(12)   59 x 84 = 4,956

(13)   563 x 74 = 41,662

(14)   43 x 20 = 86 x 10 (T)

(15)   63 x 30 = 63 x 15 + 15 (F)

(16)   99 x 11 = 990 + 99 (T)

(17)   9800 x 120 = 1,176,000

(18)   90 x 80 x 50 = 360,000

(19)   5 x 68 x 2 = 680

(20)   50 x 94 x 2 = 9400

81	÷	9	=	9
24	÷	8	=	3
21	÷	3	=	7
45	÷	5	=	9
56	÷	7	=	8
42	÷	6	=	7
63	÷	9	=	7
32	÷	8	=	4
35	÷	7	=	5
54	÷	6	=	9
40	÷	8	=	5
28	÷	7	=	4
72	÷	9	=	8
48	÷	6	=	8
30	÷	6	=	5
36	÷	9	=	4
24	÷	4	=	6
27	÷	3	=	9
18	÷	6	=	3
64	÷	8	=	8

PRACTICE12: DIVISION WITHOUT REMAINDER

(1) $\frac{400}{8} = 50$

(2) $\frac{720}{9} = 80$

(3) $\frac{4200}{70} = 60$

(4) $\frac{6300}{90} = 70$

(5) $\frac{4500}{90} = 50$

(6) $\frac{8412}{4} = 2103$

(7) $\frac{4200}{60} = 70$

(8) $\frac{3500}{70} = 50$

(9) $\frac{6005}{5} = 1201$

(10) $\frac{640480}{80} = 8006$

(11) $19352 \div 59 = 328$

```
         328
59) 19352
   - 177 ↓
     165
   - 118 ↓
       472
     - 472
       000
```

(12) $14202 \div 27 = 526$

```
         526
27) 14202
   - 135 ↓
      70
    - 54 ↓
      162
    - 162
      000
```

PRACTICE 13: DIVISION WITH REMAINDER

(1) $\frac{100}{6}$ = 16 Remainder 4

(2) $\frac{100}{7}$ = 14 Remainder 2_

(3) $\frac{100}{8}$ = 12 Remainder 4_

(4) $\frac{402}{5}$ = 80 Remainder 2

(5) $\frac{400}{3}$ = 133 Remainder 1

PRACTICE 14: NUMBERS

(1) (a)1, 2, 5, 10, 25, 50
     (b) 1, 2, 3, 4, 5, 6, 10, 12, 15, 20, 30, 60

(2) (a) 5
     (b)10

(3) (a)2^3 x 3 x 5
     (b)2^2 x 3^2 x 5

(4)
     (a)   2 x 3 x 5

(5)
     (b)2^3 x 3^2 x 5^3

(6) 24,30,36,42,48,54,60,66

(7) (a)16, (b)18 (c)60

(8) (a)100 (b)100

(9) 1,2,3,5,7,11,13,17,19,23, 29

(10) 1,4,9,16,25

(11) 1,8,27

PRACTICE 15: FRACTIONS

(1)

(2) $\frac{1}{5}$

(3)

Mixed fraction	Improper fraction
$6\frac{1}{4}$	$\frac{25}{4}$
$3\frac{5}{6}$	$\frac{23}{6}$

(4)
   (a) $\frac{18}{72} = \frac{1}{4}$
   (b) $\frac{21}{56} = \frac{3}{8}$
   (c) $\frac{24}{32} = \frac{3}{4}$

(5)
   (a) $\frac{2}{3}, \frac{14}{21}, \frac{16}{24}$
   (b) $\frac{4}{5}, \frac{24}{30}, \frac{36}{45}$

(6) $\frac{2}{5} \quad \frac{1}{2} \quad \frac{7}{10}$ $[\frac{4}{10} \quad \frac{5}{10} \quad \frac{7}{10}]$

(7) $\frac{3}{10} \quad \frac{1}{4} \quad \frac{1}{5}$ $[\frac{6}{20} \quad \frac{5}{20} \quad \frac{4}{20}]$

(8) (b) $\frac{18}{21}$

(9) (c`) $\frac{30}{48}$

(10)

Statement	True	False
$8 = \frac{1}{8}$		✓
$9 = \frac{9}{1}$	✓	
$\frac{4}{5} = \frac{4}{5} x \frac{7}{7}$	✓	
$\frac{3}{8} = \frac{3}{8} \div \frac{5}{5}$	✓	

(11)

(i) $\frac{2}{3} + \frac{1}{3} = 1$

(ii) $\frac{1}{2} + \frac{1}{4} = \frac{3}{4}$

(iii) $\frac{1}{6} - \frac{1}{8} = \frac{1}{24}$

(iv) $\frac{2}{7} + \frac{4}{9} = \frac{18+28}{63} = \frac{46}{63}$

(v) $1 + \frac{1}{6} =$

$\frac{6}{6} + \frac{1}{6} = \frac{7}{6} = 1\frac{1}{6}$

(vi) $3\frac{1}{2} - 1\frac{3}{4} =$

$\frac{7}{2} - \frac{7}{4} = \frac{14-7}{4} = \frac{7}{4}$

$= 1\frac{3}{4}$

(vii) $\frac{1}{2} + \frac{1}{3} + \frac{1}{4} =$

$\frac{6+4+3}{12} = \frac{13}{12} =$

$1\frac{1}{12}$

(viii) $\frac{1}{5} + — = 1$

$— = \frac{1}{1} - \frac{1}{5} =$

$\frac{5-1}{5} = \frac{4}{5}$

(ix) $\frac{1}{7} + — = \frac{1}{6}$

$— = \frac{1}{6} - \frac{1}{7} =$

$\frac{7-6}{42} = \frac{1}{42}$

(x) $3 - — = \frac{1}{8}$

$— = 3 - \frac{1}{8} =$

$\frac{24-1}{8} = \frac{23}{8}$

(xi) $\frac{2}{5} + — + \frac{1}{4} = 1$

$— = 1 - \frac{2}{5} - \frac{1}{4} =$

$\frac{20-8-5}{20} = \frac{7}{20}$

(12)

(i) $\frac{2}{3} \ x \ \frac{9}{10} = \frac{3}{5}$

(ii) $1\frac{1}{9} \ x \ \frac{3}{5} =$

$\frac{10}{9} x \frac{3}{5} = \frac{3}{5}$

(iii) $8 \ x \ \frac{3}{4} = 6$

(iv) $\frac{54}{63} \ x \ \frac{14}{72} = \frac{1}{6}$

(v) $\frac{2}{5} \div \frac{4}{15} =$

$\frac{2}{5} x \frac{15}{4} = \frac{3}{2} = 1\frac{1}{2}$

(vi) $1\frac{1}{6} \ x \ 1\frac{1}{5} =$

$\frac{7}{6} x \frac{6}{5} = \frac{7}{5} = 1\frac{2}{5}$

(13)

(i) $\frac{5}{6} \ x \ — = \frac{2}{3}$

$— = \frac{2}{3} \div \frac{5}{6} =$

$\frac{2}{3} x \frac{6}{5} = \frac{4}{5}$

(ii) $— \div \frac{4}{9} = \frac{27}{12}$

$— = \frac{27}{12} x \frac{4}{9} = 1$

(iii) $\frac{1}{2} \ x \ \frac{2}{3} \ x \ — = \frac{4}{5}$

$\frac{1}{3} x — = \frac{4}{5}$

$— = \frac{4}{5} \div \frac{1}{3} =$

$\frac{4}{5} x \frac{3}{1} = \frac{12}{5} = 2\frac{2}{5}$

PRACTICE 16: MORE PRACTICE

(1) $\frac{1}{4} + \frac{1}{4} = \frac{2}{4} = \frac{1}{2}$

(2) $\frac{2}{15} + \frac{1}{5} = \frac{2+3}{15} = \frac{5}{15} = \frac{1}{3}$

(3) $\frac{2}{3} + \frac{3}{4} = \frac{8+9}{12} = \frac{17}{12} = 1\frac{5}{12}$

(4) $1\frac{1}{2} + 2\frac{3}{4} = 3\frac{2+3}{4} = 3\frac{5}{4} = 4\frac{1}{4}$

(5) $2\frac{1}{5} - 1\frac{3}{10} = \frac{11}{5} - \frac{13}{10} = \frac{22-13}{10} = \frac{9}{10}$

(6) $3\frac{1}{5} - 1\frac{2}{5} = \frac{16}{5} - \frac{7}{5} = \frac{9}{5} = 1\frac{4}{5}$

(7) $\frac{2}{25} \times 7\frac{1}{2} = \frac{2^1}{25^5} \times \frac{15^3}{2^1} = \frac{3}{5}$

(8) $\frac{18}{12} \times \frac{8}{6} =2$ [try to work out]

(9) $\frac{1}{10} \times \frac{15}{2} = \frac{1}{10^2} \times \frac{15^3}{2} = \frac{3}{4}$

(10) $\frac{4}{5} \div \frac{2}{15} = \frac{4}{5} \times \frac{15}{2} = 6$

(11) $3\frac{3}{4} \times \frac{5}{8} = \frac{15}{4} \times \frac{8}{5} = 6$

PRACTICE 17: DECIMALS

(1)

0.2	>	0.02
0.5	=	0.50
0.3	=	0.30
0.07	<	0.6
0.9	>	0.10
0.08	<	0.80
0.12	<	0.21

(2) 0.10, 0.11, 0.300, 0.80, 0.9

(3)

Statement	True	False
$0.01 = \frac{0.1}{100}$		✓
$0.03 = \frac{3}{100}$	✓	
$0.6 \times 0.7 = \frac{6 \times 7}{100}$	✓	
$0.8 \times 0.9 = \frac{0.1}{\frac{8 \times 9}{100}}$		✓

(4)

(i) $0.8 + 0.9 = 1.7$

(ii) $0.68 + 1.7 = 2.38$

(iii) $4.15 + 9 = 13.15$

(iv) $1.90 - 0.34 = 1.56$

(v) $1 + 0.25 = 1.25$

(5)

(i) $0.3 \times 4 = 1.2$

(ii) $0.5 \times 0.6 = 0.3$

(iii) $9 \times 1.8 = 16.2$

(iv) $6.7 \times 8.9 = 59.63$

(v) $1.2 \times 400 = 480$

106

(vi) $0.36 \div 4 = 0.09$

(vii) $1.23 \div 3 = 0.41$

(viii) $4.836 \div 6 = 0.806$

(ix) $4.2 \div 800 =$
         0.00525

(x) $4.2 \div 700 = 0.006$

PRACTICE 18: MORE PRACTICE

(1)

(i) $0.35 = \dfrac{35}{100} = \dfrac{7}{20}$

(ii) $0.05 = \dfrac{5}{100} = \dfrac{1}{20}$

(2)

(i) $\dfrac{4}{5} = 0.8$

(ii) $\dfrac{1}{50} = 0.02$

(3)

	fraction	decimal
$1\frac{1}{2} + 2\frac{1}{4}$	$3\frac{3}{4}$	3.75
$3\frac{2}{5} - 1\frac{3}{5}$	$1\frac{4}{5}$	1.8
$\frac{1}{4} \times \frac{2}{5}$	$\frac{1}{10}$	0.1
$2\frac{1}{2} \times \frac{1}{10}$	$\frac{1}{4}$	0.25
$\frac{3}{4} \div 1\frac{1}{4}$	$\frac{3}{5}$	0.6

(4)

$\dfrac{0.03}{0.03} = \dfrac{3}{3}$	True
$\dfrac{0.05}{0.5} = \dfrac{5}{5}$	False
$\dfrac{0.12}{0.15} = \dfrac{12}{15}$	True
$\dfrac{0.01}{0.1} = \dfrac{1}{10}$	True
$\dfrac{0.12}{0.6} = \dfrac{12}{60}$	True

(5)

(i) $\dfrac{0.3}{0.03} = \dfrac{30}{3} = 10$

(ii) $\dfrac{0.12}{0.06} = \dfrac{12}{6} = 2$

(iii) $\dfrac{0.15}{0.03} = \dfrac{15}{3} = 5$

(iv) $\dfrac{0.1}{0.01} = \dfrac{10}{1} = 10$

(v) $\dfrac{15}{0.05} = \dfrac{1500}{5} = 300$

PRACTICE 19: PERCENTAGES

(1)   (a)

$$= \frac{number\ of\ triangles}{total\ number\ of\ shapes} \times 100\%$$

(b) $\frac{6}{20} x 100\% = 30\%$

(c) $\frac{14}{20} x 100\% = 70\%$

(2)   (i) $\frac{12}{40} x 100\% = 30\%$

        (ii) $\frac{28}{40} x 100\% = 70\%$

(3)   Let's T be the number of teacher and S be the number of students. Then, 25% of (T + S) = 10 →

$\frac{25}{100}$x(10 + S) = 10 →

S = $\frac{10x100}{25}$ - 10 = 40 − 10 = 30

(4) Number of non-convertible cars = 20 − 3 = 17. Then, % of non convertible cars = $\frac{17}{20}x100\% = 85\%$

(5) 52% of total students = 26

→ $\frac{52}{100}$ x total students = 26

→ total students = $\frac{26x100}{52}$=50

(6)

Fractions	Decimal	Percentage
$\frac{4}{5}$	0.8	80%
$\frac{3}{25}$	0.12	12%
$\frac{13}{100}$	0.13	13%
$\frac{1}{5}$	0.2	20%
$\frac{9}{20}$	0.45	45%
$\frac{1}{20}$	0.05	5%

(7) $0.5=\frac{5}{10}, \frac{1}{10}, \frac{4}{5} = \frac{8}{10}, 0.3=\frac{3}{10}$
$\frac{1}{10}, \frac{3}{10}, \frac{5}{10}, \frac{8}{10}$ highest to lowest:
$\frac{4}{5}, 0.5, 0.3, \frac{1}{10}$

(8)
$\frac{9}{10}, \quad 0.4 = \frac{4}{10}, \quad \frac{7}{10}, \quad 0.2 =$
$\frac{2}{10}, \quad \frac{3}{5} = \frac{6}{10}$

Then, lowest to highest: = 0.2, $0.4, \frac{3}{5}, \frac{7}{10}, \frac{9}{10}$

(9) 50kg + 30% of 50kg
50kg + $\frac{30}{100}$ x 50kg
50kg + 15kg = 65kg

(10) No.
If 40$ increased by 20%, it would become:
40$ + 20% of 40$
40$ + $\frac{20}{100}$ x 40$
40$ + 8$ = 48$
If 48% decreased by 20%, it would become:
48$ - 20% of 48$
48$ - $\frac{20}{100}$ x 48$
48$ - 9.6$ = 38.4$ [not 40$ as it was before]

(11) (i)Discount = 30% of 50€ = $\frac{30}{100}$ x 50€ = 15€
(ii)sale price = 50€ - 15€ = 35€

(12) £12 + 2% of £12
£12 + $\frac{2}{100}$ x 12 = £12.24

(13) 55% of 65 million = $\frac{55}{100}$ x 65 million = 35.75 millions = 35,750,000 female

(14) % playing cricket = 100 − (40+25+20) = 15%
Member playing crickets = 15% of 200 = $\frac{15}{100}$ x 200 = 30

(15) % of student walking to school =

$\frac{students\ walking\ to\ school}{total\ students}$ x 100% =

$\frac{50-(20+12+3)}{50}$ $x100\%$ =

$\frac{15}{50}$ $x100\%$ = 30%

PRACTICE 20: BODMAS

(1) $(59 - 39) \div \frac{5}{3}$ = 12

(2) $3(\frac{500}{4} - 25)$ = 300

(3) (47 + 13) x 70% = 42

(4) $\frac{2}{1+(10-3)}$ x 4 = 1

(5) 4 + (10 - 4) x 1.5 = 15

(6) $5 + (12 - 8) \times \frac{32}{48} \times 2$ = 12

(7) 6 + 3 x 2 = 6 + 6 = 12

(8) 7 x 4 - 3 = 28 - 3 = 25

(9) 8 x 5 - 3 x 4 = 40 - 12 = 28

(10) 8 x (5 - 3) x 4 = 8x2x4=64

PRACTICE 21: THE SYSTEM

(1) $20 \times \frac{10 \times 2}{4}$ = 100

(2) $40 \times \frac{2 \times 3}{8}$ = 30

PRACTICE 22: RATIO AND PROPORTION

(1) (i)$\frac{AB}{BC} = \frac{4}{1}$ → AB = 4BC

AC = AB + BC, AC = 600cm

→ 600 = AB + BC

4BC + BC = 5BC

→ BC = $\frac{600}{5}$ = 120cm

(ii)AB = 4BC = 4 x 120 = 480cm

(2) (i)$\frac{BC}{AC} = \frac{2}{7}$ → 7BC = 2AC

BC = 14ft

→ 7 x 14 = 2AC

→ AC = $\frac{7 \times 14}{2}$ = 49ft

AB + BC = AC

AB + 14 = 49 → AB = 49 − 14 = 35ft

(ii)AC = 49ft (calculated)

(3) $\frac{field\ width}{field\ lenth} = \frac{model\ width}{model\ length}$

$\frac{field\ width}{120cm} = \frac{2.5cm}{6cm}$

→ field width =

$\frac{2.5cm}{6cm} x120cm = 50cm$

120cm

(4) Model = $\frac{1}{100}$ x actual

7cm = $\frac{1}{100}$ x actual

→ actual = 7cm x 100

700cm = 7m

(5) $\frac{500mls(0.5\ litres)}{5000\ litres} = \frac{15\ toads}{toads\ in\ pond}$

Toads in pond =
$\dfrac{15\,toads \times 5000\,litres}{0.5\,litres} =$
150,000 toads

(6) (i) $\dfrac{\dfrac{20g}{200mls(0.2\,ltres)}}{\dfrac{sugar\ content}{1.5\,litres}} =$

Sugar content =
$\dfrac{20g}{0.2\,litres} \times 1.5\,litres = 15g$

(iii) $\dfrac{\dfrac{20g}{0.2\,litres}}{\dfrac{75g}{drink\ volume}} =$

Drink volume =
$\dfrac{75g \times 0.2\,litres}{20g} = 0.75$ litres =
750mls

(7) Scale = $\dfrac{\dfrac{1}{100,000}}{\dfrac{distance\ on\ map}{distance\ on\ ground}} =$

Distance on ground = 6cm
x 100,000 = 600,000cm =
600,000cm x
$\dfrac{1m}{100cm} \times \dfrac{1km}{1000m} = 6km$

PRACTICE 23: ROUNDING

(1)

Round to:	Nearest digits
5.4	5
$7\frac{3}{4}$	8
Round to:	Nearest tens
46	50
73	70
Round to:	Nearest hundreds
539	500
262	300
Round to:	Nearest thousands
5,464	5,000
4,820	5,000
Round to:	Nearest ten thousands
24,642	25,000
82,976	83,000
Round to:	Nearest millions
2,612,431	3,000,000
7,429,658	7,000,000

(2)

Round 6,735,829 to the nearest:	
Million:	7,000,000
Ten thousand	6,740,000
Thousand	6,736,000
Hundred	6,735,800
Ten	6,735,830

(1) $a + a + a + b + b = 3a + 2b$

(2) $4a + 5b - 7a - 7b = -3a - 2b$

(3) $2a + 6b - 5a - 5 = -3a = 5b$ or $5b - 3a$

(4) $20 \times a = 20a$

(5) $2b \times 3b = 6b^2$

(6) $16 \times \frac{3b}{4} = 12b$

(7) $3a \times 4bc = 12abc$

(8) $\frac{4ab}{2b} = 2a$

(9) $\frac{4a^2 b}{2ab^2} = \frac{2a}{b}$

(10) $\frac{4a \times 5b}{20a} = b$

(11) $\frac{(a+b) \times (a \times b)}{(a+b)} = a \times b$

(12) $\frac{(a+b) + (a+b) + (a+b)}{a+b} = 2(a+b)$

(13) $\frac{4b^2}{2b} = 2b$

(14) $\frac{4(a+b)^2}{2(a+b)} = 2(a+b)$

(1)

(i) $a(b + c) = ab + ac$

(ii) $3a(4b - 2c) = 12ab - 6ac$

(iii) $(m + n)(m - n) = m^2 - n^2$

(iv) $(2p + 3)(4p - 5) = 8p^2 + 2p - 15$

(v) $(a + b)(a + b) = a^2 + 2ab + b^2$

(vi) $(a + b)(a - b) = a^2 - b^2$

(vii) $3(a + \frac{2b}{9}) = 3a + \frac{2b}{3}$

(viii) $12(b - \frac{5c}{4}) = 12b - 15c$

(2)

(i) $ab + ac = a(b+c)$

(ii) $3abc - 6ac = 3ac(b - 2)$

(iii) $12ab^2 + 6a^2 b = 6ab(2b + a)$

(iv) $3ab - 12ab^2 = 3ab(1 - 4b)$

(v) $4a^2 b^2 c + 20abc = 4abc(ab + 5)$

(3)

(i) $5(a + \frac{b}{10}) = 5a + 2b$

(ii)

$$7a + b = 7\left(a + \frac{b}{7}\right)$$

(4)

(i) $\dfrac{4a+8b}{2a+4b} = \dfrac{4(a+2b)}{2(a+2b)} = 2$

(ii) $\dfrac{5a+20b+a-2b}{4a+10b-a-b} =$

$\dfrac{6a+18b}{3a+9b} =$

$\dfrac{6(a+3b)}{3(a+3b)} = 2$

(iii) $\dfrac{5n-2m}{m+n} - 3 =$

$\dfrac{5x5-2x2}{2+5} - 3 =$

$\dfrac{21}{7} - 3 = 0$

(iv) $\dfrac{(m+1)(n+1)}{n+m} x28 =$

$\dfrac{(2+1)(5+1)}{2+5} x28 =$

$\dfrac{3x6}{7} x28 = 72$

(v) $\dfrac{m^2+n^2}{m+n} = \dfrac{2^2+5^2}{2+5} =$

$\dfrac{4+25}{7} = \dfrac{29}{7} = 4\dfrac{1}{7}$

(5)

Statement	True	False
A + B = B + A	✓	
A − B = B − A		✓
A x B = B x A	✓	
$\dfrac{A}{B} = \dfrac{B}{A}$		✓
$\dfrac{A+B}{B} = A$		✓
$\dfrac{A x B}{A} = B$	✓	
$\dfrac{4a+5b}{4a} = \dfrac{4a}{4a} + 5b$		✓
$\dfrac{4a+5b}{4a} = \dfrac{4a}{4a} + \dfrac{5b}{4a}$	✓	
$\dfrac{6a x b}{c} = \dfrac{6a}{c} x \dfrac{b}{c}$		✓
$\dfrac{6a x b}{c} = \dfrac{6a}{c} x b$	✓	

(2)

Statement	expression
Sum of numbers	X + Y
Difference of numbers	X − Y
Product of numbers	XY
First number is three times the second number	X = 3Y

PRACTICE26: EXPRESSIONS

(1)

(i) $3m - n = 3x2 - 5$

$= 6 - 5 = 1$

(ii) $\dfrac{3n-3m}{n-m} = \dfrac{3(n-m)}{(n-m)} = 3$

112

(3)

Statement	Expression
You had £50 and you gave some money away	50 - M
You had some money and you gave £5 away	M - 5
You had some money and you add the same amount of money into your pocket	M + M = 2M
You had money and you add half of the amount of money you had into your pocket	$\frac{3M}{2}$ [M + $\frac{1}{2}$M]

(1) $192 + x = 243$

$\rightarrow x = 243 - 192 = 51$

(2) $497 - 2x = 321$

$\rightarrow x = \frac{497-321}{2} = \frac{176}{2} = 88$

(3) $\frac{q}{70} = 80$

$\rightarrow q = 80 \times 70 = 5600$

(4) $2q + 35 = 9q$

$\rightarrow 9q - 2q = 35$

$7q = 35 \rightarrow q = \frac{35}{7} = 5$

(5) $1 + \frac{q}{4} = 5$

$\rightarrow \frac{q}{4} = 4 \rightarrow q = 4 \times 4 = 16$

(6) $\frac{5q}{4} + \frac{1}{4} = \frac{1}{3}$

$\rightarrow \frac{5q+1}{4} = \frac{1}{3}$

$\rightarrow 5q + 1 = \frac{4}{3}$

$\rightarrow 5q = \frac{4}{3} - 1 = \frac{4}{3} - \frac{3}{3} = \frac{1}{3}$

(7) $\frac{12+q}{q} = 5$

$\rightarrow 12 + q = 5q$

$\rightarrow 4q = 12$

$\rightarrow q = \frac{12}{4} = 3$

(8) $2(4q + 5) + 10 = 36$

[÷ by 2 both sides]

$\rightarrow 4q + 5 + 5 = 18$

$\rightarrow 4q + 10 = 18$

$\rightarrow 4q = 8$

$\rightarrow q = \frac{8}{4} = 2$

(9) $\frac{25}{20+3q} = 1$

$\rightarrow 25 = 20 + 3q$

$\rightarrow 3q = 5 \rightarrow q = \frac{5}{3} = 1\frac{2}{3}$

(10) $\frac{2q+1}{3q-5} = \frac{7}{4}$

  → $4(2q + 1) = 7(3q - 5)$

  $8q + 4 = 21q - 35$

  → $4 + 35 = 21q - 8q$

  $39 = 13q$

  → $q = \frac{39}{13} = 3$

(11) (i) $T = 50 + 4n$

  $T = 50 + 4(6)$

  $50 + 24 = 74$

  (ii) $170 = 50 + 4n$

  → $4n = 170 - 50 = 120$

  → $n = \frac{120}{4} = 30$

(12) $3a + 6b = 30$ [factorise]

  $3(a + 2b) = 30$

  → $a + 2b = 10$ $[\frac{30}{3}]$

(13) $2a + b = 1$ [factorise]

  $2(a + \frac{b}{2}) = 1$

  → $a + \frac{b}{2} = \frac{1}{2}$

(14) $4p + 6q = 20$ [factorise]

  $4(p + \frac{6q}{4}) = 20$

  $4(p + \frac{3q}{2}) = 20$

  → $p + \frac{3q}{2} = 5$ $[\frac{20}{4}]$

(15) (i) $12A + 3B = 9$

  [divide both sides by 3]

  → $4A + B = 3C$

(ii) $A + B = C$

[multiply both sides by 5]

→ $5A + 5B = 5C$ or $5(A + B) = 5C$

(iii) $\frac{A}{2} + B = C$

[multiply both sides by 2]

→ $A + 2B = 2C$

(iv) $\frac{3A}{2} + \frac{5B}{4} = \frac{5C}{8}$

[multiply each both sides by 8]

→ $12A + 10B = 5C$

(v) $\frac{3A}{4} + \frac{5B}{2} = \frac{4C}{3}$

[multiply each both sides by 12]

→ $9A + 30B = 16C$

PRACTICE 28: TWO EQUATIONS

(1) $4p = 12$ → **p = 3**

  [substitute the value of p
  in the equation:
  $3p + r = 11$]

  Then,

  $3(3) + r = 11$

  → **r = 2** [11 - 9]

114

(2) $6p = 1.8 \rightarrow$ **$p = 0.3$**
[substitute the value of p
in the equation:
$2p + r = 0.8$]
$2 \times 0.3 + r = 0.8$
$\rightarrow$ **$r = 0.2$** $[0.8 - 0.6]$

(3) $\frac{80}{p} = 20 \rightarrow$ **$p = 4$** $[\frac{80}{20}]$
[substitute the value of p
in the equation:
$2p + 3r = 23$]
$\rightarrow 2 \times 4 + 3r = 23$
$\rightarrow 3r = 15$
$\rightarrow$ **$r = 5$**

(4) $\frac{p}{3} + \frac{2p}{3} = 1$
[multiply by 3 both sides]
$\rightarrow p + 2p = 3$ **$p = 1$**
[substitute the value of p
in the equation:
$2p + 5r = 22$]
$\rightarrow 2 \times 1 + 5r = 22$
$\rightarrow 5r = 20 \rightarrow$ **$r = 4$**

(5) 20% of p = 24
Then, $\frac{20}{100} \times p = 24$
$\rightarrow$ **$p = 120$** $[24 \times \frac{100}{20}]$
[substitute the value of p
in the equation:
30% of p + 40% of r=96]
Then,
$\frac{30}{100} \times 120 + \frac{40}{100} \times r = 96$
$\rightarrow 36 + \frac{2}{5} \times r = 96$

$\rightarrow r = (96 - 36) \times \frac{5}{2}$
$= 60 \times \frac{5}{2} = 30 \times 5$
$\rightarrow$ **$r = 150$**

(6) $20p = 1000$
$\rightarrow$ **$p = 50$** $[\frac{1000}{20}]$
[substitute the value of p
in the equation:
$4p + 5r = 7700$]
$4 \times 50 + 5r = 7700$
$200 + 5r = 7700$
$5r = 7700 - 200$
$5r = 7500$
$r = 1500$ $[\frac{7500}{5}]$

(7) If $A + B = X$
$A - B = Y$

	Tick two
$A + B = X + Y$	
$2A = X + Y$	✓
$2A + 2B = X + Y$	
$A = \frac{X+Y}{2}$	✓

(8) $A + B = 20$
$A - B = 10$
[add two equation
together]
$A + B + A - B = 20 + 10$
  $2A = 30$
$\rightarrow$ **$A = 15$**
[substitute the value of A
in the equation: $A - B = 10$]

Then, 15 − B = 10

→ **B = 5** [15 - 10]

(9) 3 pencils cost £1.20

2 pencils and one rubber cost £1.00

Let the cost of one pencil be p and the cost of rubber be r

Then,

3p = £1.20 → **p = £0.40**

2p + r = £1.00

2 x £0.40 + r = £1.00

→ **r = £0.2** [£1.00 - £0.8]

(10)

Ω+ Ω+ Ω+ Ω = 52

→ 4 Ω = 52 → **Ω = 13**

α+ α+ Ω+ α+ α+ Ω = 58

→ 2 Ω + 4 α = 58

→ 2 x 13 + 4 α = 58

→ 26 + 4 α = 58

→ 4 α = 32 [58 − 26]

→ **α = 8** $[\frac{32}{4}]$

(11) The weight of 5 big blocks is equal to the weight of 6 small blocks.
The weight of one big block is 3 kg. Required: Weight of one small block.

Let the weight of big block be b and the weight of small block be s.

Then, 5b = 6s

b = 3kg

then, 5 x 3 = 6 x s

→ s = $\frac{5 \times 3}{6}$ = 2.5kg

(1) (i)Let the number be x, then; $x + \frac{x}{2} + \frac{x}{4} = 175$

(ii)[multiply each side by 4]

→ 4x + 2x + x = 175 X 4

→ 7x = 700 → x = 100

(2) (i)Let the number be x, then; $2x + \frac{x}{2} + 10 = 20$

(ii)multiply each side of by 2, then; 4x + x + 20 = 40

→ 5x = 20 → x = 4 $[\frac{20}{5}]$

(3) (i)Let T = total cost and R = number of rides, then; T = 2 + 3R

(ii)T = 2 + 3 x 5 = 17

(iii)30 = 2 + 3 x R

→ 28 = 3R → R = 9r1

(nine rides and £1 remain)

(4) (i)Let T is the cooking time and W is the weight of chicken in kg, then;

T = 30 + 25W

(ii)T = 30 + 25 x 3 = 105 minutes (0r 1 hour and 45 minutes)

(iii)2hours 35 minutes = (120 + 35) minutes = 155 minutes, then;

T = 30 + 25W

155 = 30 + 25W

$\rightarrow$ W = $\frac{155-30}{25}$ = $\frac{120^{24}}{25^5}$ = 4.8 kg

(5) 15 pens = £4.50 [£10 − £5.50]

$\rightarrow$ pen = $\frac{£4.5}{15}$ = £0.30 (or 30p)

(6) Bradley buy:

3apples = £1.2

$\rightarrow$ apple = $\frac{£1.2}{3}$ = £0.40 or 40p

Kendis buy:

2apples + 2bananas = £1.40

Then,

2 x £0.4 + 2bananas = £1.40

£0.8 + 2bananas = £1.4

$\rightarrow$ 2bananas = £0.6 [1.4 - 0.8]

Banana = £0.30 or 30p

(7) [Target is to calculate the cost of each kg of rice]

Bag A:

5kg = £5.50

$\rightarrow$ kg = £1.10 [$\frac{5.50}{5}$]

Bag B:

3kg = £3.60

$\rightarrow$ kg = £1.20 [$\frac{3.60}{3}$]

So bag A is the best buy

PRACTICE 30: MORE PRACTICE

(1)

a = $\frac{1}{2}$b $\rightarrow$ b = 2a

[substitute b with 2a into the other equation] , then

a + 2a = 90

$\rightarrow$3a = 90 $\rightarrow$ a = 30

b = 2a = 2 x 30 = 60

(2) The sum of a and b is 40. b is three times of a.

    (i)   Equations:

a+ b = 40
b = 3a

    (ii)   [substitute b with 3a into the other equation]

→ a + 3a = 40

→ 4a = 40 → a = 10

Then, b = 3 x 10 = 30

(3) The difference of a and b is 75. a is half of b.

    (i)   Equations:

b − a = 75
$a = \frac{b}{2}$

    (ii)   Since $a = \frac{b}{2}$,

Then, b = 2a

[substitute b with 2a into the other equation]

2a − a = 75

→ a = 75

Then,

b = 2 x 75 = 150

(4) The sum of a and b is 450. a is double of b.

    (i)   Equations:

a + b = 450
a = 2b

    (ii)   [substitute a with 2b]

→ 2b + b = 450

→ 3b = 450

→ b = 150

Then,

a = 2 x 150 = 300

(5) The sum of a and b is 100. b is 20 less than a.

    (i)   Equations:

a + b =100
b = a − 20

    (ii)   [substitute b with a − 20 into the first equation]

→ a + a − 20 = 100

→ 2a = 120

→ a = 60

Then,

b = 60 − 20 = 40

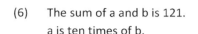

(6) The sum of a and b is 121.
a is ten times of b.
    (i)   Equations:

$a + b = 121$
$a = 10b$

    (ii)   [substitute a with 10b into the first equation]
        $\rightarrow 10b + b = 121$
        $\rightarrow 11b = 121$
        $\rightarrow b = 11$
        Then,
        $a = 10 \times 11 = 110$

(7) The sum of a and b is 70. a is 12 more than b.
    (i)   Equations:

$a + b = 70$
$a = b + 12$

    (ii)   [substitute a with b + 12 into the first equation]
        Then,

$b + 12 + b = 70$

$\rightarrow 2b = 58$

$\rightarrow b = 29$

Then,

$a = 29 + 12 = 41$

(8) Jamal and Jaden together weight 80kg. Jaden alone weight 26kg.
Required: Jamal's weight

Let Jamal's weight be J and Jaden's weight be D.
Then, $J + D = 80kg$
And $D = 26kg$
[substitute D = 26kg in the first equation]
Then, $J + 26kg = 80kg$
$\rightarrow J = 80kg - 26kg = $ **54kg**

(9) One bag of potatoes and one bag of rice both together cost £12. A bag of rice costs as three times as a bag of potatoes.
Requared:
    (i)   Cost of a bag of potatoes.
    (ii)   Cost of a bag of rice.

Let be the cost of a bag of potatoes be p and the cost of a bag of rice be r.

Then, $p + r = £12$

$r = 3p$

[substitute r with 3p in the first equation]

Then, $p + 3p = £12$

$\rightarrow$ (i)$4p = £12 \rightarrow$ **p = £3**

(ii) r = 3 x £3 = **£9**

(10) The sum of Salum's age and Fatmas age is 14 years. Fatma is 4 years younger than Salum.
Required:
(i)   Salum's age
(ii)   Fatma's age

Let Salum's age be s and fatma's age be f.

Then, s + f = 14 years

And f = s − 4 years

[substitute f with s − 4 in the first equation]

s + s − 4 year(i)**s = 14 years**

2s = 18 years → s = 9 years

(ii)f = 9 years − 4 years = **5 years**

(11) I bought 6 pens and 3 rubbers for £2.40. I then bought 3 rubbers for 60p.
Required: cost of a pen.
Let the cost of one pen be p and the cost of one rubber be r.
Then, 6p + 3r = £2.40
3r = £0.6 → r = £0.2
[substitute r with £0.2 in the first equation]

Then, 6p + 3 x £0.2 = £2.40
→ 6p = £2.40 − £0.6 = £1.80
→ **p = £0.30**

(12) There are two pieces of string: red and blue. The piece of blue string is 4 times longer than the piece of red string.

Two pieces of string are joined end to end. The total length is 20cm.

Required:

(i)   The length of red string
(ii)   The length of blue string

Let the length of red string be r and the length of blue string be b.

Then, b = 4r

    b + r = 20cm

[substitute b with 4r into the second equation]

Then, 4r + r = 20cm

→ 5r = 20cm → (i)**r = 4cm**

(ii)**b = 4 x 4cm = 16cm**

(13) The weight of strawberries' bag and the weight of grapes' bag is 3.4kg.
The weight of strawberries' bag is 1.6kg less than the weight of grapes' bag.
Required:
(i) The weight of strawberries' bag
(ii) The weight of grapes' bag

Let the weight of strawberries' bag is s and the weight of grapes' bag be g.

Then, s + g = 3.4kg

s = g - 1.6kg

[substitute s with 1.6kg in the first equation]

Then, g – 1.6kg + g = 3.4kg

2g = 3.4kg + 1.6kg = 5.0kg

→ g = 2.5kg

s = 2.5kg – 1.6kg = 0.9kg

so, (i) **s = 0.9kg** and

(ii) **g = 2.5kg**

(1)

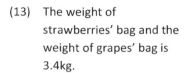

Quantity	Units
Time	$kg \div \dfrac{kg}{m^3}$
Distance	$second \; x \; \dfrac{metre}{second}$
Weight	$\dfrac{kg}{m^3} \; x \; m^3$
Volume	$meter \div \dfrac{meter}{second}$
Money	$kg \div \dfrac{kg}{\$}$

(2) (i) 10€ = 12$
$$90€ = \frac{90€ \; x \; 12\$}{10€} = 108\$$$
(ii) 12$ = 10€
$$60\$ = \frac{60\$ \; x \; 10€}{12\$} = 50€$$

(3) (i) 10 miles = 16km
50 miles =
$$\frac{50 \; miles \; x \; 16km}{10 \; miles} = 80km$$
(ii) 16km = 10 miles

400km =
$$\frac{400km \; x \; 10 \; miles}{16km} = 250 \; miles$$

(4) (i) 1 litre = 0.22 gallon
10 litres = 10 x 0.22
gallon = 2.2 gallons
(ii) 100 litres = 22
gallons

(5) 200g + 4kg = 0.2kg + 4kg =
4.2kg

(6) 0.3kg + 150g = 300g +
150g = 450g

(7) 0.1 litre + 250mls = 100mls
+ 250mls = 350mls

(8) 2 litres + 700mls = = 2
litres + 0.7 litre = 2.7 litres

(9) £0.2 + 60p = 20p + 60p =
80p

(10) 80p + 75p =155p = £1.55

(11) $\frac{5\ litres}{20mls} = \frac{5000mls}{20mls} = 250$

(1)

Shape	Triangle name
	Equilateral
	Right angled
	Scalene
	Isosceles

(2) $25cm^2 - 12cm^2 = .13cm^2$

(3) (i) (14cm x 14cm) –
$154cm^2 = 196cm^2 -$
$154cm^2 = 42cm^2$
(ii) $\frac{14}{2} = 7cm$

(4) (i) (84m x 84m) – $1386m^2$
$= 7056m^2 - 1386m^2$
$= 5670m^2$
(ii) $\frac{84}{4} = 21m$

(5) 5cm x 4cm = $20cm^2$

(6) (i) area = $\frac{1}{2}$bh = $\frac{1}{2}$ x 4cm x
3cm = 6cm2
(ii) perimeter = 3cm + 4cm
+ 5cm = 12cm

(7)

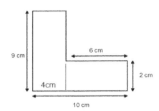

Area = 9cm x 4cm
+6cm x 2cm = 48cm^2
Perimeter = (9 + 10 + 2 +
6+ 7 + 4)cm = 38cm

(8)

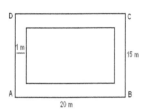

Dimensions of the picture
(20 − 2) by (15 − 2) =
18m by 13m
(i)Area of the picture
= 18m x 13m = 234m^2
(ii)Perimeter of the picture
= (18 + 13)m x 2 = 62m

(9)

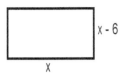

Perimeter = 28cm
→ (x + x − 6) x 2 = 28cm
→ 2x − 6 = 14
→ x = 10cm = length
width = 10cm − 6cm = 4cm
Area = 10cm x 4cm
= 40cm^2

(10)   Let the width of the
rectangle be w and its
length is w + 5.

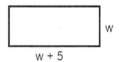

Perimeter = 50 cm
→ (w+ w + 5) x 2 = 50cm

→2w + 5 = 25

w = 10cm = width

Length = w + 5 = 10 + 5 = 15cm

Area = 10cm x 15cm = 150cm^2

PRACTICE 33 ANGLES

(1)

Angles		Type
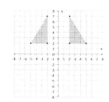		Obtuse angle
		Acute
		Right angle
		Reflex angle

(2)

Clock face	Pointer moved:	Angle size
12 o'clock	12	360°
1 o'clock	1	30° $[\frac{360}{12}]$
7 o'clock	7	210° [30 x 7]

(3)   30 x 5 = 150°

(4)   90°

(5)   270° [90 x 3]

PRACTICE 34: CO-ORDINATES

(1)

Quadrant		Signs
I		(+x, +y)
II		(-x, +y)
III		(+x, -y)
IV		(-x, -y)

(2)   B(10, 2)
       A(10, 20+2) = (10,22)
       D(30,2)
       C(30,22)
       M(20, 10+2) = (20, 12)

PRACTICE 35: TRANSFORMATION (reflection and translation)

(1) A(5, 1)   B(-4, 3)
    C(-1, -3)   D(4, -5)
(2) (i)A(5, 1) → A'(5, -1)
    (ii)B(-4, 3) → B'(4, 3)
    (iii)C(-1, -3) → C'(1, -3)
    (iv)D(5, -5) → D'(-5, -5)
(3) (i)A(5, 1) → A'(3, 4)
    (ii)B(-4, 3) → B'(2, -5)
    (iii)C(-1, 3) → C'(1, -2)
    (iii)D(5, -5) → D'(4, -3)

(4)

124

(5)

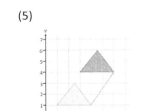

PRACTICE 36: HANDLING DATA

(1)

Data you collected from the internet	Primary Data
Data you collected from the library	Secondary data
You counted and recorded the type of the car passing on the road	

(2)

Weight of students	Discrete data
Number of the students	
Height of the plants	Continuous data

(3)　(a)Mean =

$$\frac{sum\ of\ marks}{number\ of\ students} = \frac{730}{10} = 73$$

(b)Median is the middle number after arranging them in order. If there are two middle numbers, calculate their average.

<u>50, 60, 60, 70</u>, 70, 80, <u>80, 80, 90, 90</u>

So median = $\frac{70+80}{2}$ = 75

(c) Mode = the mark that occurred the most = 80 (3 times)

(d) Range = maximum − minimum = 90 − 50 = 40

(e)

Marks	Tally	frequency
50	|	1
60	|	2
70	||	2
80	|||	3
90	||	2

(f)

number of students

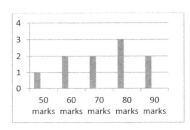

(4)　4 + 2 = 6 children

QUESTION BANK

(1) $2439 + 638 = 3077$

(2) $1,000,000 - 1 = 999,999$

(3) $5 - 8 = -3$

(4) $72 - 123 = -51$

(5) Rule: +12

$\underline{14}$, 26, 38, $\underline{50}$, 62, 74, $\underline{86}$

(6) $42 \times 53 = 2,226$

(7) $8349 \times 76 = 634,524$

(8) $3832 \div 4 = 958$

(9) $16638 \div 47 = 354$

(10) $4263 - \underline{3465} = 798$

(11) $\frac{1}{6} - \frac{1}{9} = \frac{1}{18}$

(12) $\frac{4}{5} \div 28 = \frac{1}{35}$

(13) $1\frac{2}{3} + 2\frac{3}{4} = 4\frac{5}{12}$

(14) $2\frac{3}{5} x 25 = 65$

(15) $2\frac{1}{2} \div 1\frac{4}{5} = 1\frac{7}{18}$

(16) $27 \times 1.6 = 43.2$

(17) $400 \times 2.4 = 960$

(18) $14.5 \div 4 = 3.625$

(19) $1.45 \div 0.4 = 3.625$

(20) 30% of £160 = £48

(21) (i) $4 - (-3) = 4 + 3 = 7°$

(ii) $-3 - 8 = -11°C$

(22)

Clock reading	Digital reading
	✓ 13:35
	7:35
	✓ 1:35
	3:35

(23)

Time spent to:	
Get prepared for school	30 minutes
Walk to school	15 minutes
Time you are suppose to be at school	08:45
Time to wake up	**08:00**

(24)

1^1 : 50

2 : 45

4 : 35

(25) 55 minute

(26)

	To the nearest tens
12.521	10.000
125.21	130.00
1252.1	1250.0

(27) $M - (1.25 + 1.6) = \frac{3}{4}M$

$M - 2.85 = \frac{3}{4}M$

$M - \frac{3}{4}M = 2.85$

Multiply both sides by

$4M - 3M = 2.85 \times 4$

$M = 11.40$

(28) Let M be the money that Rose has started with

$M - (2.20 + 1.80) = \frac{2}{3}M$

$M - 4 = \frac{2}{3}M$

Multiply both sides by 3

$3M - 2M = 12$

$M = 12$

(29) $3x = 96 \rightarrow x = 32$ $[\frac{96}{3}]$

$2x + 2y = 100$

$2 \times 32 + 2y = 100$

$64 + 2y = 100$

$2y = 100 - 64 = 36$

$2y = 36 \rightarrow y = 18 \ [\frac{36}{2}]$

(30) $6x = 24 \rightarrow x = 4$ $[\frac{24}{6}]$

$3x - 4y = 2$

$3 \times 4 - 4y = 2$

$\rightarrow y = 2.5 \ [\frac{10}{4}]$

(31) 4apples = 1.2$

$\rightarrow$ apple = 0.3$ $[\frac{1.2}{4}]$

2apples + 3bananas = 2.1$

$2 \times 0.3 + 3bananas = 2.1$

3bananas = 1.5

Banana = 0.5$

(32) 6cm − (1.4cm + 2.4cm)

= 6cm − 3.7cm = 2.3cm

(33) Change = £5 − 4 x £0.6

= £5 - £2.4 = £2.6

(34) 3 bags = £10 - £7.90

3bags = £2.1

Bag = £0.7 $[\frac{2.1}{3}]$

(35) (i) 69 x 75 = 69 x (76 − 1)

= 69 x 76 − 69

= 5244 − 69

=5,175

(ii) 69 x 78 = 69 x (76 + 2)

= 69 x 76 + 69 x 2

= 5144 + 138

= 5,282

MINI FLASH CARDS

CUT THEM OUT AND KEEP PRACTICING

12 x 3	48 ÷ 12
8 x 5	72 ÷ 6
9 x 7	54 ÷ 9
12 x 5	64 ÷ 8
9 x 8	45 ÷ 9
7 x 6	36 ÷ 6
4 x 12	48 ÷ 12
7 x 8	42 ÷ 7
9 x 6	32 ÷ 8
6 x 12	49 ÷ 7

4	36
12	45
6	63
8	60
5	72
6	42
4	48
6	56
4	54
7	72

CONGRATULATION

AIMED TO BUILD STRONG

MATHEMATICAL FOUNDATION

FOR

SECONDARY SCHOOL

KNOWLEDGELAND STUDY PATH

PRE-SCHOOL

AGE 4

→ YEAR 1

AGE 5

→ YEAR 2

AGE 6

KS1

PREPARATION

AGE 5-6

YEAR 3

AGE 7

→ YEAR 4

AGE 8

→ YEAR 5

AGE 9

→ YEAR 6

AGE 10

KS2

PREPARATION

AGE 7-10

KS3

PREPARATION

AGE 11-14

GCSE

PREPARATION

AGE 14-16

Printed in Great Britain
by Amazon

57495191R00078